One-Minute Devotions for the Church Musician

Cycle C

One-Minute
DEVOTIONS

for the Church Musician

CYCLE C

Nancy M. Raabe

MorningStar
MUSIC PUBLISHERS

ISBN: 978-0-944529-55-3

*This volume is dedicated to my husband Bill,
in gratitude for the breadth of his love
and the extravagance of his encouragement.*

*Lord, grant that I in ev'ry place
may glorify thy lavish grace
and serve and help my neighbor.*

Martin Schalling, "Lord, Thee I Love With All My Heart"

LIVING INTO OUR CALL

Devotions for the Church Musician

Church music is not merely a profession. Neither is it an avocation nor a hobby. Rather, it is a *ministry*, one which is as critical to the church's vitality as is ordained ministry.

We are musicians of the church because of the power of God, "who saved us and called us with a holy calling, not according to our works but according to his own purpose and grace" (2 Timothy 1:9). Whether as directors, keyboardists, singers, instrumentalists or composers, through God's gift of music we proclaim the good news of the resurrection of Jesus and his victory over death to a world in need. Because death no longer has dominion over us, the world and everything in it is forever changed. We are no longer people of fear; we are people of hope. This is the substance of our song.

It is my hope that this series of devotional books will invite the reader more deeply into what it means to be called to ministry through music. Tied to the three-year cycle of weekly lessons assigned by the Revised Common Lectionary, these brief devotions are grounded in the Gospel reading for each week and are designed to be used during the week preceding the Sunday on which that reading will be heard.

These devotions are exegetical rather than experiential. That is, their purpose is to draw out the meaning of each reading, rather than to have us "read in" our own meaning based on our own experiences. Once the exegetical meaning is grasped, it is then up to each of us how we relate that meaning to our lives. Many entries end with a question, whether explicit or implied, about how our intersection with the text can strengthen our sense of call in our own unique situation.

There are two primary ways the devotions can be used.

At the beginning or end of choir rehearsals

- Purchase copies of the book for your choir members so that all may follow along.

- Hand out copies of the Gospel lesson for the coming Sunday to all present (or pass around Bibles). If there is time, have someone read through the lesson; if not, choir members may simply have it in hand to refer to if necessary.

- Invite someone to read the devotion and its closing prayer.

- Allow one or two minutes for responses and discussion.

- If time permits, read aloud the hymn verse quoted at the end of the devotion and invite your singers to reflect silently for a few moments on how the verse echoes the devotion they have just heard. Then ask whether anyone can identify the tune most commonly associated with those words. Over time this may encourage your singers to pay closer attention to the texts of each week's hymns, and to grasp how theology is transmitted through hymnody.

In your own devotional time

- Spend time with the assigned lesson before turning to the devotion. Read the lesson slowly, making note of words or phrases that catch your attention. Spend a few minutes in contemplative silence with images or thoughts that arise.

- Read through the devotion.

- Journal about your experience with the text and your response to the devotion. Perhaps your own intersection with the text was significantly different from that suggested by the devotion. What might the Spirit therefore be calling forth from you?

- Locate the entire hymn from which a verse has been excerpted. Read through the verses and use them as means of prayer.

This book is also ideal for church council or other congregational meetings, although you may choose to adapt the text of the devotion so that it addresses all who are present.

There are other activities that can also lead the musicians of your congregation to think theologically.

- Make sure your choir members are familiar with the concept of the Revised Common Lectionary and have access to the readings for the entire three-year cycle. An excellent online resource provided by the Vanderbilt Divinity Library is located at http://lectionary.library.vanderbilt.edu/. For those without online access, you may find the three-volume *Lectionary for Worship* (Cycles A, B and C) published by Augsburg Fortress in your church library or office. The concept behind the lectionary is nicely explained by the Evangelical Lutheran Church in America's web site at http://www.elca.org/Growing-In-Faith/ Worship/Lectionary.aspx. Make copies for those who cannot go online to read it. You might expand this into a useful church newsletter item.

- Speaking of newsletters, do you have a monthly column? If not, why not start one, using it to reflect on aspects of your congregation's worship through music?

- When you introduce an anthem, talk about why you chose it. In what way does it resonate with the assigned lessons for the week in which it will be sung? Identify one or two lines of the text that bear the weight of this meaning. The same can be done for the hymns chosen for each week.

- As you work through the anthem, point out what aspects of the music do (or do not) enhance one's understanding of the words being sung, and why.

- If the devotion for the week happens to be closely related to the anthem (which is possible since the devotion is tied to the Gospel reading), schedule the devotional time at the end of the rehearsal rather than at the beginning, and ask for comments on those connections.

- Armed with this reflection on the Gospel lesson ahead of time, your singers may challenge themselves in the service itself to discern the common theme that connects all the assigned lessons for the day. Did the sermon address this theme? They can be also be encouraged to pay special attention to the way that the psalm serves as a bridge from the Old Testament reading to the Gospel reading.

Yours in Christ,

Nancy Raabe
Bexley, Ohio
March 2012

References

Raymond E. Brown, *The Gospel According to John, I–XII and XIII–XXI* (*The Anchor Bible,* Volumes 29 and 29A). New York: Doubleday, 1966.

Joel B. Green, *The Gospel of Luke.* Grand Rapids: William B. Eerdmans Publishing Company, 1997.

Timothy Lull, *Martin Luther's Basic Theological Writings.* Minneapolis: Augsburg Fortress Publishers, 2005.

HEIGHTENED ALERT

First Sunday of Advent: Luke 21:25–36

Many find themselves puzzled by the apocalyptic imagery in the lessons assigned for Advent. Yes, we are preparing for Jesus' coming—but shouldn't we be talking about the coming of a baby born in a humble setting with all the attendant adjectives (poor, meek, mild), rather than a return from the clouds marked by cosmic signs and a terrestrial roar such as that described in Luke 21?

Consider that instead the lectionary invites us not necessarily to ponder detail but to assume an attitude. In Advent, our entire being is drawn together not in fear and awe but in *readiness*. Whatever is to come, we are to prepare ourselves now. We take our cue from v. 36: "be alert at all times…"

Whether it concerns Jesus' birth or Jesus' final return, we are to align our hearts, minds and lives into a position of right relationship with God. What does this state of heightened alertness consist of? We may reach back into Luke 12 for more: Seek God's kingdom; do not be afraid; keep our lamps lit; be good stewards of what God has given us; and, to invoke 1 Thessalonians 5, pray without ceasing. And let all your music be prayer.

God of wisdom, teach us to take note of signs of your advent in our midst so that we may focus our hearts and minds only on you.

*Then fling the gates wide open
to greet your promised king!*

Frans Mikael Franzén, "Prepare the Royal Highway"
Text © 1978 *Lutheran Book of Worship*, admin. Augsburg Fortress

DECK THE HALLS (NOT)

Second Sunday of Advent: Luke 3:1-6

How invigorating it is to arrive once again at Luke 3:4, that magnificent summons to our deepest Advent preparations:

The voice of one crying in the wilderness:
"Prepare the way of the Lord, make his paths straight."

Luke cites Isaiah as his source, but there is a telling difference from what we find in Isaiah 40. There, the prophet announces that "a voice cries out, 'Prepare the way for the Lord in the wilderness.'" But in Luke it is the one calling, not the one coming, who is positioned in the wilderness.

Can we receive this, busy musicians that we are of whom much is required in this season, as an exhortation to enter the wilderness as we prepare to welcome the Lord?

This requires us to vigorously oppose the movement of our culture. All around us lights are being strung, trees trimmed, decorations hung, and businesses and workplaces decked out in glaring shades of red and green.

But the practice of contemplative prayer, which creates in us the space in which to welcome the Christ child, requires little of us. All we need is a quiet corner, a willing heart and perhaps a candle. Here in our little wilderness, stripped of all excess, we may breathe in the crisp air of the Spirit and ponder how to make straight the path that Jesus, resplendent in love, will blaze into our hearts.

God of love, we pray that we are able to discover
in the midst of our Advent wilderness
the peace of Christ which the world cannot give.

───────────────────

His is no earthly kingdom; it comes from heav'n above.
His rule is peace and freedom and justice, truth, and love.

Frans Mikael Franzén, "Prepare the Royal Highway"
Text © 1978 *Lutheran Book of Worship*, admin. Augsburg Fortress

CHARITY AND CHURCH GROWTH

Third Sunday of Advent: Luke 3:7–18

What does it look like, this baptism of repentance for the forgiveness of sins which John proclaimed in "all the region around the Jordan" in last week's reading? It is spelled out in this week's verses with bracing clarity.

Deeply stirred by John's words, the crowd eagerly demands to know what they should do and peppers him with questions. Patiently addressing each of their situations, John replies that they are to perform acts of charity using the means they have at hand.

In our post-resurrection world, let us put ourselves in their place. Each act of charity has three implications. It expresses our love of God, our gratitude for God's merciful love, and the advent of God's kingdom on earth. This is how we respond to the coming of Emmanuel, "God with us."

But these gestures of love are also instruments of community. Writes Joel Brown, "by definition the forgiveness of sins has a profound communal dimension; as sin is the means by which persons exclude themselves from community with and the community of God's people, so forgiveness marks their restoration to the community."[1]

This is the true answer to the riddle of church growth. About the earliest Christian community, we read in Acts 2 that "Day by day, as they spent much time together in the temple, they broke bread at home and ate their food with glad and generous hearts, praising God and having the goodwill of all the people. And day by day the Lord added to their number those who were being saved."

Merciful God, pour your love into our hearts so that through acts of love we may be more closely knit together in community.

*Day by day, I know you will provide me
strength to serve and wisdom to obey;
I will seek your loving will to guide me
o'er the paths I struggle day by day.*

Carolina Sandell Berg, tr. Robert Leaf, "Day by Day,"
Text © 1992 Augsburg Fortress

MIRRORS OF GRACE

Fourth Sunday of Advent: Luke 1:39–45 (46–55)

From Luke, we know Mary to have been a deeply reflective person.

When Gabriel says to her, "Rejoice, favored one! The Lord is with you," she "pondered what sort of greeting this might be." After all the excitement of that first Christmas, when amazement had spread through the countryside following the shepherds' news of the Savior's birth, Luke tells us that "Mary treasured all these words and pondered them in her heart." And after the boy Jesus' experience in the temple, Luke writes again that "His mother treasured all these things in her heart."

Here in the Magnificat, Mary's song of gratitude prompted by Elizabeth's blessing, we find her most stirring act of reflection. She praises God's dramatic acts across the ages; she integrates into this panorama her own story ("for he has looked with favor on the lowliness of his servant"); and she recognizes that the imminent birth inaugurates the reign of God and leads toward the consummation of God's purpose for the world ("Surely, from now on all generations will call me blessed; for the Mighty One has done great things for me, and holy is his name. His mercy is for those who fear him from generation to generation….").

Amid the busy-ness of this Advent season, how can we cultivate a similar attitude of reflection? One way is to be attentive to the work of the Spirit. What acts of love, generosity and encouragement do we observe among those in our midst? Seize these as opportunities for reflection and treasure their meaning in your heart.

> **God of grace, alert us to reflections of love in our midst
> as signs of your Spirit among us.**

---

*When this old world drew on toward night,
you came; but not in splendor bright,
not as a monarch, but the child
of Mary, blessed virgin mild.*

9th century Latin hymn, "Creator of the Stars of Night,"
Text © 1940 Church Pension Fund

SOUNDING JOY

Nativity of Our Lord I (Christmas Eve): Isaiah 9:2–7

"Wonderful Counselor!" "Mighty God!" "Eternal Father!" "Prince of Peace!" Applied to the birth of Christ, these ringing titles given to the Messiah by the prophet Isaiah announce to us the reign of God on earth.

What does this mean in a world where brokenness still surrounds us, where even on this blessed night sin retains its grip and multitudes languish in darkness without adequate food, clothing or shelter?

It means that it is not up to us to restore the broken order: God in Christ through the Spirit has already done that. Instead of "fixing" the world, we are to use our life to proclaim the reality of God's kingdom. In ways both large and small, our service to the world testifies to what God has already done.

Our privilege as musicians is to serve as sounding boards for the mighty acts of God. Let our lives resonate with the saving grace that comes to us through the Christ child!

God, make us worthy servants in the proclamation of your kingdom.

Silent night, holy night!
Son of God, love's pure light
radiant beams from your holy face,
with the dawn of redeeming grace,
Jesus, Lord at your birth,
Jesus, Lord at your birth.

Joseph Mohr, tr. John F. Young, "Silent Night, Holy Night"

MUSIC MINISTRY AS PROPHETIC WITNESS

Nativity of Our Lord (Christmas Dawn): Luke 2:(1–7) 8–20

As musicians of the church, we are not merely hired hands who carry out various tasks concerning the church's worship life. We are prophetic witnesses to the inbreaking of God's kingdom. As such it is a component of our calling to observe, to absorb, and to reflect.

We may look again to Mary as our model. The shepherds on that first Christmas night were excited by the great news, and all those to whom they made it known were amazed—they were impressed but lacked understanding. "But Mary treasured all these words," Luke tells us, "and pondered them in her heart."

This quiet reflection prepared her to fully absorb the meaning of what Simeon was to tell them in the temple not long after. Speaking directly to Mary he says, "This child is destined for the falling and the rising of many in Israel, and to be a sign that will be opposed so that the inner thoughts of many will be revealed..." (Luke 2:34–35a).

The music we choose, how we offer it in worship, and the way in which we compassionately conduct all aspects of our ministry helps the church discern the nature of its mission in the world.

God of inspiration, let us live through your Spirit
into the vocation of proclamation through music to which you have called us.

Come, then, let us hasten yonder;
here let all, great and small,
kneel in awe and wonder;
love him who with love is yearning;
hail the star that from far
bright with hope is burning.

Paul Gerhardt, tr. Catherine Winkworth, "All My Heart Again Rejoices"

OBEDIENCE AND GOD'S PURPOSE

First Sunday after Christmas: Luke 2:41–52

Here we encounter a touching story about the boy Jesus, the only window in the Gospels onto his boyhood and upbringing.

We are given to understand that he is raised in a devout family which adheres to the religious customs and attempts to fulfill God's purpose for their lives. However, we note here a surprising shift concerning God's purpose for this particular child. His family clearly considers it to be God's will that Jesus return with them to Nazareth. But unbeknownst to them Jesus remains in the temple and later informs his parents that *that* was God's purpose: "Did you not know that I had to be in my Father's house?"

This is intriguing but not revelatory. What happens after that is key. Jesus does not turn into a rebellious youth. Instead his life becomes one of obedience: "Then he went down with them and came to Nazareth, and was obedient to them. His mother treasured all these things in her heart. And Jesus increased in wisdom and in years and in divine and human favor."

How can this attitude inform our ministry? Feeling under-appreciated and misunderstood, we may be tempted at times to denounce the authorities and go our separate ways. But God has called each of us to our current position, whether or not the church has sanctioned it as a "call." How can we make known God's purpose for our congregation within the structures of authority into which we have been placed?

God of grace, help us to discern what is your will for us
and to develop the confidence to trust only in you.

My faithful God, on ev'ry road
you know the way unfolding
and my hand you are holding.

Samuel Rodigast, tr. Martin A. Seltz, "What God Ordains Is Good Indeed"
Text © 2000 Augsburg Fortress

METANOIA

Second Sunday after Christmas: John 1:(1–9), 10–18

In the frenetic rush of getting ready for Christmas, and in the inevitable exhaustion that follows, we may temporarily lose sight of the purpose of our work as musicians of the church. Verse 12 of this passage serves as a welcome reminder: "But to all who received him, who believed in his name, he gave power to become children of God…"

We are engaged in the business of changing minds and hearts from unbelief to belief through the transcendent language of music. It is not up to *us*, of course, to do that changing. That is God's work. But if we give ourselves over to music's expressive power, God will be able to use each hymn, each anthem, each prelude and postlude to bring about the kind of metanoia (change of heart) that can open each person fully to the love of Christ.

Lord of all of hopefulness, commit our hearts, minds,
and voices to the transformative power of music.

Lord of all eagerness, Lord of all faith,
whose strong hands were skilled at the plane and the lathe:
be there at our labors, and give us, we pray,
your strength in our hearts, Lord, at the noon of the day.

Jan Struther, "Lord of All Hopefulness"
Text © Oxford University Press

FAITH-FILLED FOLLOWING

The Epiphany of Our Lord: Matthew 2:1–12

It is interesting to ponder how God is able to work through situations which might seem on the surface to be contrary to divine purpose.

Surely the magi, as perceptive and thoughtful individuals, sensed Herod's fearfulness at the news that a rival king had been born. They must have recognized his dark purposes when the frightened ruler dramatically convened all the chief priests and scribes, demanding to know where this child had been born.

Yet they were obedient to his wishes. They provided him with the information he asked for about when the star had appeared, and dutifully set out at his command to search for the child. At that time they probably did not know what would come of their discovery in terms of Herod's fanatic desire to locate and kill the infant king. One imagines them having heated discussions on the long journey: "It's great if we find him—then what?"

At some point along the way, however, God warned them in a dream not to return to Herod. The warning did not save the lives of innocent young children in and around Bethlehem, but it did save that of Jesus.

Sometimes we may find ourselves asked to carry out tasks which might seem contrary to God's will, Perhaps we have little choice initially other than to go along. Let the story of the magi assure us that the Spirit will provide us with whatever we need to serve the Lord faithfully.

Loving God, give us hearts of faith
so that in our obedience to you we find perfect freedom.

Amen! Amen!
Come, Lord Jesus! Crown of gladness!
We are yearning
for the day of your returning.

Philipp Nicolai, tr. *Lutheran Book of Worship*, "O Morning Star, How Fair and Bright"
Text © 1978 *Lutheran Book of Worship*, admin. Augsburg Fortress

BAPTISM WITH FIRE

The Baptism of Our Lord: Luke 3:15–17, 21–22

John's pronouncement in 3:16, "He will baptize you with the Holy Spirit and with fire," distinguishes Jesus' baptism as superior to the baptism of repentance with which John was serving God. But it also points us forward in Luke to a challenging verse in Luke 12:49: "I came to bring fire to the earth," Jesus says, "how I wish it were already kindled!"

Baptism with fire surely refers to the outpouring of the Holy Spirit at Pentecost, where tongues of fire come to rest on those present, much as the dove at his baptism descended onto Jesus (in the Greek, the preposition translated as "on" is the same in both passages).

In Luke 12, Jesus longs for that transformative event. How may we, through our music, inspire in others that same zeal for transformation and new life which is at the heart of the Christian experience?

***God of renewal, kindle in our hearts the fire of your love
and enable us to share that with others through the gifts you have given us.***

---

*Teach me to love you as your angels love,
one holy passion filling all my frame:
the baptism of the heav'n-descended dove,
my heart an altar, and your love the flame.*

George Croly, "Spirit of God, Descend upon My Heart"

MUSIC AS PROCLAMATION

Second Sunday after the Epiphany: John 2:1–11

Here it is fruitful to focus not on water being changed to wine but on the exchange between Mary and Jesus which precedes the miracle. In response to Mary's observation that the wine has run out, Jesus responds, "Woman, what has this concern of yours to do with me? My hour has not yet come." What does he mean?

John scholar Raymond Brown suggests that here Jesus' mother represents the church, which has no role in Jesus' ministry but is called into action at the hour of his passion, death and resurrection. "Then she will appear at the foot of the cross to be entrusted with offspring whom she must protect in the continuing struggle between Satan and the followers of the Messiah."[2]

How can we position ourselves at the foot of the cross and invite others to that same place? The hymns we sing, the way our settings underscore the meaning of the text, and way in which we invite people to reflect on those hymns through our preludes and postludes all have the ability to call others into communion with Jesus' suffering, his death, and his glorious resurrection. Music is a powerful form of proclamation.

Nurturing God, you give us signs and wonders
as testimonies of your saving power.
Make us worthy servants in our proclamation of salvation
by grace through faith.

As we worship, grant us vision,
till your love's revealing light
in its height and depth and greatness
dawns upon our quickened sight.

Albert F. Bayly, "Lord, Whose Love in Humble Service"
Text © Oxford University Press

POVERTY AND GRACE

Third Sunday after the Epiphany: Luke 4:14–21

"The Spirit of the Lord is upon me, because he has anointed me to bring good news to the poor." (Luke 4:18)

In the aftermath of natural disasters, there inevitably emerge countless stories of how faith in God provided hope to people in their darkest hours.

In normal circumstances of life the mainstream media does not engage in faith-oriented reporting in their main news sections, but in crises these stories always find a prominent place. Can we consider that, in these journalistic acts, the risen Jesus is continuing to do that which he announced to his home congregation in Nazareth, in the first reported incident in his ministry: to bring good news to the poor?

For we too are the poor, not just the distressed, displaced Haitians, Chinese, Japanese, Syrians, or countless other souls languishing in sickness, strife and despair whose governments failed to protect them. We are poor in faith, poor in compassion, poor in our commitment to the cross and all that it calls us to become. We hunger and thirst for salvation as eagerly as do the displaced persons for nourishment and physical comfort.

In stories of people rescued from crises by their faith, the result is often an outpouring of aid from sympathetic readers. If we were able to communicate our spiritual poverty through music in a way that invited the Spirit's involvement, who knows what forms of spiritual disaster relief might be poured into our midst—and on into the lives of other suffering souls?

***God of the poor, bring us into solidarity
with our suffering sisters and brothers throughout the world
so that we may take on their poverty as our own.***

---

*Finish then thy new creation,
pure and spotless let us be;
let us see thy great salvation
perfectly restored in thee.*

Charles Wesley, "Love Divine, All Loves Excelling"

PIONEERS OF COMPASSION

Fourth Sunday after the Epiphany: Luke 4:21–30

This reading offers us a cautionary tale about how easy it is to get wrapped up in our own community and forget about the less fortunate outside our doors.

Here, in Luke's powerful telling of Jesus' return to his home town, those in the synagogue are first entranced and then enraged as he makes clear the meaning of his reading from Isaiah: "…he has anointed me to bring good news to the poor…" What really upsets them is that Jesus points out that their prophets Elijah and Elisha were sent to minister to not only those in the lowliest classes—widows and lepers—but also to Gentiles.

Caring for those in our own community is important. But how many of your congregation's activities are in-house affairs? The potluck following this or that meeting…the youth retreat…pastries during the fellowship hour…the building campaign…how much time is left over for those in desperate need and who might not even be Christian?

How in our music can we encourage people to be pioneers of compassion who will venture outside the comfort of our church building?

> *God of justice, use us in your service*
> *to break down barriers which separate your people*
> *so that all may know the blessings of your grace.*

> *The poor ones of the world await the dawn of hope,*
> *when justice will shine and make oppression flee.*
> *The empty hands of all are raised to you, Lord God:*
> *Oh, set us free!*

Juan A. Espinosa, tr. Martin Seltz, "The People Walk"
Text © 1972, 1998 Juan A. Espinosa, admin. OCP Publications

DEEP WATER

Fifth Sunday after the Epiphany: Luke 5:1–11

"Put out into the deep water and let your nets down for a catch."
(Luke 5:4)

Often we find ourselves doggedly pursuing the same old path and not making much progress. If we pause to listen, though, we might hear Jesus addressing to us a prophetic exhortation just as he did to Peter. How would we respond? Peter is obstinate at first: "Master, we have worked all night long but have caught nothing." Then: "Yet if you say so, I will let down the nets."

How does this apply to our music ministry? Perhaps we've been recycling the same repertoire of hymns for years without a discernible spark. Perhaps we've been stuck in the same liturgy for twenty years. Month after month, year after year, our nets come up empty.

Take a moment to listen to Jesus. What might he be telling us? Where is *our* deep water? God only knows what awaits us there.

God of infinite love, show us how our music might be a net
by which we, too, may become fishers of people.

───────────────

You know full well what I have, Lord:
neither treasure nor weapons for conquest,
just these my fish nets and will for working.

Cesáreao Gabaráin, tr. Madeleine Forrest Marshall, "You Have Come Down to the Lakeshore"
Text © 1979 Cesáro Gabaráin, admin. OCP Publications

MINISTRY ON THE MARGINS

Sixth Sunday after the Epiphany: Luke 6:17–26

It is important to acknowledge that Jesus' famous list of blessings and woes in Luke 6 does not emerge out of ordinary circumstances. He was not instructing his disciples in the comfort of a local house or establishment. He was not teaching in the security of a local synagogue.

Instead, Jesus had just been ministering to those on society's margins: a leper, a paralytic, a tax collector, a man with a withered hand. Then, calling his 12 disciples and positioning himself on "a level place, with a great crowd of his disciples and a great multitude of people from all Judea, Jerusalem, and the coast of Tyre and Sidon" (all of whom were straining to touch him), Jesus fixes his gaze on his disciples and utters the powerful words which so clearly articulate the nature of God's kingdom on earth, then and now—truth for all who heard then, and truth for us now: *"Blessed are you who are poor, for yours is the kingdom of God...."*

Let us also seek whenever possible to attend to those on the margins, whether in our choirs, our congregations or in the world beyond the church walls. Through them we will discover that we have a capacity for ministry in the most extraordinary forms.

Gracious God, give us the boldness to venture outside our comfort zone so that we may discover new dimensions of your love.

Onward in his footsteps treading,
trav'lers here, our home above,
full of faith and hope and love,
let us do our Savior's bidding.
Faithful Lord, with me abide;
I shall follow at your side.

Sigismund von Birken, tr. *Lutheran Book of Worship*, "Let Us Ever Walk with Jesus"
Text © 1978 *Lutheran Book of Worship*, admin. Augsburg Fortress

LEAP OF FAITH

Seventh Sunday after the Epiphany: Luke 6:27–38

"But I say to you that listen, Love your enemies, do good to those who hate you, bless those who curse you, pray for those who abuse you" (Luke 6:27–28).

As hard as we try, it seems that only the most saintly among us are capable of these acts on a regular basis.

But let's read on in this passage and think about how some of the seemingly easier prescriptions are still far beyond our grasp. We demand gratitude: "I bailed her out but got not even a simple thank-you in return!" We demand repayment: "He said he'd pay me back but so far I haven't seen a dime!" We demand that others share our burdens: "I've done all the work and she has barely lifted a finger."

But what good is it, Jesus says accusingly, if we confine our actions only to those by which we expect to be rewarded in a certain way?

Let us take a leap of faith and let go of our expectations for how our acts of kindness should be repaid. God may have some amazing surprises in store for us.

God of compassion, free us to love and serve you with all our hearts.

———————————————

Lord, you can help when earthly armor fails us;
Lord, you can save when deadly sin assails us;
and, in the day when hell itself appalls us,
grant us your peace, Lord.

Matthäus von Löwenstern, tr. Philip Pusey, "Lord of Our Life"

TREASURE OF THE HEART, PART I

Eighth Sunday after the Epiphany: Luke 6:39–49

In the church, as in the rest of life, we encounter those who say one thing and do another. Perhaps our pastors or parishioners praise us to our face but work to undermine us behind our backs. But in the church, as in the rest of life, we are called to a higher path, one which involves complete transformation in Christ with utter consistency between the inner and outer person. This is the purpose of Jesus' list of "parables" in this reading.

With them we recall Paul's words in Colossians 3:12–15: "As God's chosen ones, holy and beloved, clothe yourselves with compassion, kindness, humility, meekness, and patience. Bear with one another and, if anyone has a complaint against another, forgive each other; just as the Lord has forgiven you, so you also must forgive. Above all, clothe yourselves with love, which binds everything together in perfect harmony. And let the peace of Christ rule in your hearts, to which indeed you were called in the one body."

And, Paul adds, "be thankful."

We can't control the actions of others but we do have jurisdiction over our own inner and outer lives. Let us concentrate on the "good treasure of the heart" (Luke 6:45) and our ministry will flourish out of that abundance.

God of new life, show us how to walk as children of your light.

What joy to know, when life is past,
the Lord we love is first and last,
the end and the beginning!

Philipp Nicolai, tr. *Lutheran Book of Worship*, "O Morning Star, How Fair and Bright"
Text © 1978 *Lutheran Book of Worship*, admin. Augsburg Fortress

HEARING IS BELIEVING

Transfiguration of Our Lord: Luke 9:28–36

Our culture is visually oriented, but as musicians we inhabit the world of sound. How refreshing, then, to find in Luke's account of Jesus' transfiguration the news that hearing trumps seeing!

In the first part of this reading, the disciples have plenty to gaze at. Verse 30 even begins with the imperative to "Look!" However, the disciples do not know what to make of what they see, judging by Peter's awkward offer to build three dwellings. Instead it is God's voice in verse 35, "This is my Son, my chosen: *Listen* to him!" which opens the gates of insight. Luke doesn't specifically tell us that they achieved some understanding but implies it, adding that the disciples told no one what they had seen.

Let us make the most of every opportunity to put music to service as a gateway to the mysteries of the Triune God.

God of all senses, use the work of our hands to make your truth known through the world of sound.

With Moses and Elijah nigh
the incarnate Lord holds converse high,
and from the cloud, the Holy One
says, "This is my beloved Son."

Sarum, 15th century, tr. John Mason Neale, "Oh, Wondrous Type! Oh, Vision Fair!"

BETWEEN THE NOTES

Ash Wednesday: Matthew 6:1–6, 16–21

These verses from Matthew's Sermon on the Mount are particularly appropriate for those who wear their cross of ashes far into the next day. "Beware of practicing your piety before others in order to be seen by them," Jesus cautions, "for then you have no reward from your Father in heaven."

In a similar way we are to embrace the Christian calling to humility and compassion in our giving and service to the church. We give not to be noticed but because we love the church ("when you give alms, do not let your left hand know what your right hand is doing"). We pray not to be noticed but because we love God ("whenever you pray, go into your room and shut the door and pray to your Father who is in secret; and your Father who sees in secret will reward you").

In the same way, we offer music to God not to be praised or to impress but simply to allow others to enter into God's Word through song. For there within the notes, or rather between the notes, will be found all the treasures of heaven.

Lord, make us humble servants in all that we do.

"For where your treasure is, there your heart will be also."
For I know my transgressions, and my sin is ever before me.
Purge me with hyssop, and I shall be clean;
wash me, and I shall be whiter than snow."

Psalm 51:7

ON OUR WAY REJOICING

First Sunday in Lent: Luke 4:1–13

Luke's account of Jesus' temptation hints at what a supreme test he endured. To be in the wilderness for forty days, alone and without food, is an inconceivable hardship. But then we read in verse 13 that the devil subjected him to "every test," not just the three trials which Luke recounts in detail.

God does not desire for us to be put to such trials, but we can learn to confront the temptations we face honestly and courageously, and reach into the farthest depths of our being to respond in a way that is faithful to God. In this way our faith is increased. Then we, too, shall be able to endure whatever trials we find ourselves confronted with; and we, too, shall pass through their midst (see Luke 4:30) and go on our way.

God of limitless power, give us courage to meet the trials in our lives with faith, confidence and hope in you.

*For he will command his angels concerning you
to guard you in all your ways.
On their hands they will bear you up,
so that you will not dash your foot against a stone.*

Psalm 91:11–12

RIGHT SPIRITS

Second Sunday in Lent: Luke 13:31–35

Jesus' lament for Jerusalem touches us at the heart of our humanity: "Jerusalem, Jerusalem, the city that kills the prophets and stones those who are sent to it! How often have I desired to gather your children together as a hen gathers her brood under her wings, and you were not willing!"

We sometimes encounter similar forms of obstinacy in our congregations. These might include a fear of engaging with people who are different ethnically or socioeconomically ("they don't look like us"); levels of giving that are far below tithing ("the church is doing just fine"); a distrust of liturgical worship ("we don't want to scare away visitors"); or the reluctance to learn new hymns ("what's wrong with the old ones?").

What can we do? Lament, as Jesus did; continue to proclaim the victory of the cross; and trust in the Holy Spirit to work through our proclamation to create clean hearts and to renew right spirits.

Nurturing God, work through our music to release people from their fears so that they may become more vigorously engaged in the life of the church.

As we worship, grant us vision, till your love's revealing light in its height and depth and greatness dawns upon our quickened sight, making known the needs and burdens your compassion bids us bear, stirring us to ardent service, your abundant life to share.

Albert F. Bayly, "Lord, Whose Love in Humble Service"
Text © Oxford University Press

BEARING FRUIT

Third Sunday in Lent: Luke 13:1–9

On its own, the parable of the barren fig tree in Luke 13:6–9 seems almost inconsequential. We can begin to appreciate its significance if we consider the intensity of Luke's Chapter 12 out of which it grows.

With panoramic sweep, in that single chapter Jesus addresses the urgent need for faithfulness, detachment from possessions, preparation, vigilance, being attuned to the present, and at the outset of Chapter 13, repentance.

These qualities do not grow in us without effort on our parts. They must be cultivated in God's sight. If we think of the fig tree as our soul, the center of our spiritual life which houses the thirst for God (see Psalm 63, appointed for this day as well), Jesus is telling us that we must provide it with the nutrients it needs to bear fruit.

This takes place not just through the simple act of watering but also by means of the gritty act of digging around (verse 8)—creating, through diligent effort, the spaces into which those nutrients may be infused and then working to integrate those with the soil which surrounds it.

How may the songs that we sing and the *way* that we sing them contribute to this process, one that gets our hands dirty with the life-giving work of cultivating souls to bear fruit?

God of new life,
give us the wisdom to use the tools you have given us for your glory.

———————————

Tell how, when at length the fullness
of the appointed time was come,
Christ, the Word, was born of woman,
left for us the heav'nly home,
blazed the path of true obedience,
shone as light amidst the gloom.

Venantius Honorius Fortunatus, tr. John Mason Neale, alt.,"Sing, My Tongue"

LOST AND FOUND

Fourth Sunday in Lent: Luke 15:1–3, 11b–32

The very title by which this parable is commonly known, the "prodigal son," sends the wrong message about its meaning. This story is neither about poor stewardship nor about redemption. Rather, it is an account of a father's great joy in finding a beloved member of his family who had been lost to him. The closing verse, spoken by the father to the eldest son, sums it up: "We had to celebrate and rejoice, because this brother of yours was dead and has come to life; he was lost and has been found."

As is so often the case in the Gospels, but especially in Luke, meaning may be discerned through context. Note that this is the last of three "lost and found" stories in Luke 15 (lost sheep, lost coin), each of which concludes in joy over the recovery of that which was lost. Note also how Luke sets it up in the first verse of Chapter 15: *"Now all the tax collectors and sinners were coming near to listen to him."*

Those who had been lost, the outcasts, are drawing close to Jesus. They have been found. How much more beautiful it is, when we come to understand these three parables in Luke 15, that a human being, formerly lost, is restored to the family of God!

How may we reach out through music to the lost so that they, too, may find their way back to their Savior?

> *God of love, show us how music's transformative power*
> *may help lost souls find their way back to you.*

> *Be of good cheer, for God's own Son*
> *forgives all sins that you have done,*
> *and justified by Jesus' blood,*
> *your baptism grants the highest good.*

Gesangbuch, Collhagen, 1791; tr. August Crull, "God Loved the World"

LIVING WITHOUT FEAR

Fifth Sunday in Lent: John 12:1–8

John's story of Mary anointing Jesus with expensive perfume offers us a fine Lenten lesson in three of the "seven deadly sins"—pride, avarice and envy.

Judas objects to the use of the perfume because he self-righteously argues it should have been sold and the proceeds given to the poor. His prideful attitude is revealed in his alleged desire to perform a good work and receive accolades from it. His avarice is exposed as we learn that Judas actually was a thief and was accustomed to steal from the very pool of money he guarded. His envy is revealed as he objects to Mary's use of the expensive perfume, which prevents him from appreciating Mary's moving gesture. As an anticipation of Jesus' burial, her anointing of Jesus offers a clear expression of her faith in Jesus and in who he says he is.

Let us pray that God free us from the fear which causes us to regularly commit these same sins. Only then can we be truly present to others and recognize the Christ who lives in them. How can our music exhibit that same fearlessness?

God of hope, give us the confidence to embrace your victory of life over death in every aspect of our lives so that we are able to live without fear.

Lord, whose life in humble service bore the weight of human need,
who upon the cross, forsaken, worked your mercy's perfect deed:
we, your servants, bring the worship not of voice alone, but heart;
consecrating to your purpose ev'ry gift which you impart.

Albert F. Bayly, "Lord, Whose Love in Humble Service"
Text © Oxford University Press

SALVATION AND PRAYER

Sunday of the Passion/Palm Sunday: Luke 22:14–23:56

The Passion story is one of high drama and many facets. Its spiritual center of gravity, however, is located in struggle between God and Satan which takes place on the Mount of Olives as Jesus prays (Luke 22:39–46): "Father, if you are willing, remove this cup from me; yet, not my will but yours be done." Here Jesus faces his last great test.

Tellingly, immediately before this Jesus urges his disciples to pray so that they may not enter into the "time of trial."

Imagine if we were to find ourselves unjustly condemned to death. We might understandably think that Satan had won the day. But prayer, as Jesus reminds his disciples, is indispensable. Prayer does not just give us the strength to endure hardship, it grounds us in God's love so that Satan can have no power over us in times when we are tempted to give into despair.

We can encourage in our choirs the practice of prayer by beginning and ending each rehearsal in this way. Below is a prayer I learned from Ronald Nelson, composer of music beloved to Lutherans everywhere. I have used it for years to conclude every rehearsal.

> *God of boundless love,*
> *remind us whenever possible that prayer puts Satan to flight.*
> *Keep our hearts focused only on you.*

> *Bless us, O Lord, your servants who work in this place;*
> *what we sing with our lips, may we believe in our hearts;*
> *what we believe in our hearts, may we show forth in our lives.*
> *We ask this through your Son, Jesus Christ, our Lord.*

Anonymous

FOOT-WASHING AND SALVATION

Maundy Thursday: John 13:1–7, 31b–35

To those not familiar with the practice, the idea of foot-washing on Maundy Thursday creates consternation. For some it may be simply a matter of not wanting to display their bare feet in church. Others might be reluctant to allow someone to perform for them an act of such earthy compassion. As caretakers of our congregations, many of us know well how to give but not so well how to receive.

This same reluctance was probably behind Peter's first, impetuous response as Jesus approaches him with basin and towel: "You shall not wash my feet—ever!" But Jesus then tells him plainly that without this symbolic act, Peter will have no part with Jesus in God's eternal kingdom.

What Jesus is saying is that the foot-washing is not merely a symbol of servitude or an expression of the elimination of barriers (master/servant). It also points us to the scandal and humiliation of Jesus' death. In accepting a servant of God to wash our feet, especially on Maundy Thursday, we also accept the cross, its salvific purpose, and all that this entails. The cross is the ultimate expression of God's love for us. We receive it not only with gratitude but with eagerness to love God in return—with all our heart, all our soul and all our mind (Matt. 22:37).

Merciful God, open our hearts to receive the love you pour into our hearts through the sacrifice of your Son.

***

What language shall I borrow to thank thee, dearest friend,
for this, thy dying sorrow, thy pity without end?
Oh, make me thine forever, and should I fainting be,
Lord, let me never, never outlive my love for thee.

Paul Gerhardt, "O Sacred Head, Now Wounded"

MUSIC AND TRUTH

Good Friday: John 18:1–19:42

Jesus' rebuttal to Pilate's inquisition in John 18:36 offers us a telling model for our own response to persecution.

We may sometimes feel that we are under attack by forces we do not understand and cannot control. We object not only to the content of these accusations but to the way they are carried out. The warfare may take place behind closed doors so that we only hear about it through the grapevine, or third parties may be called into play to serve the accuser's purpose. Our instinct is to retaliate.

Notice, however, what Jesus does in response to Pilate after the prefect bluntly demands to know what Jesus has done. Jesus does not respond to the accusations nor does he defend himself. Instead he shifts to a higher plane of discourse—that of the location of the kingdom over which he reigns.

Knowing nothing of the kingdom of heaven, Pilate can only respond in terms of the world he knows: "So, you *are* a king?" Again, Jesus shifts the discourse to the higher plane. By so doing, instead of dignifying Pilate's accusations he may simply speak the truth: "You say I am a king. For this I was born, and for this I came into the world, to testify to the truth."

Can this become our model when we find ourselves under attack? Instead of merely defending ourselves, offer instead the testimony of truth concerning the nature and purpose of God's kingdom. And do this not only through words but also through music, for that universal language communicates truth more clearly than any other.

God of justice, give us the courage to always speak your truth
so that the work of your kingdom may be accomplished through us.

Tell how, when at length the fullness
of the appointed time was come,
Christ, the Word, was born of woman,
left for us the heav'nly home,
blazed the path of true obedience,
shone as light amid the gloom.

Venantius Honorius Fortunatus, John Mason Neale, alt., "Sing, My Tongue"

FAITHFUL MESSENGERS

The Resurrection of Our Lord/The Vigil of Easter: Luke 24:1–12

With the strokes of a master storyteller, Luke portrays three very different responses to the discovery of the empty tomb on Easter morning.

The majority of the disciples scoff, dismissing the women's report as "an idle tale." Peter hurries to check it out and discovers things just as they said, but is merely "amazed"—he does not know what to make of it. The women, however, comprehend. Absorbing the angels' proclamation, they recall Jesus' own words and are able to put it all together.

Each of us can identify people we know who fit all three categories in their response to the news of the Resurrection. It is particularly useful for us to consider the differences between the second and third. How easy it is for us to be like Peter, amazed by events but essentially clueless. Instead how can we be more like Mary Magdalene, Joanna, Mary the mother of James, and the others who listened to what the angels said and then thoughtfully put it all together?

Most of us do not have the benefit of angels talking to us, but there are many ways in which we can listen, ponder, and learn. These include prayer, the reading of scripture, and the thoughtful singing of hymns. Then, with time for reflection, we can assume our role as God's faithful messengers who eagerly bring to the world the news of Christ's victory over death.

God of new life, we thank and praise you
for your great victory over death and the grave.
Enlighten our hearts with the power of your truth
so that we may be worthy messengers of the resurrection.

True God, he first from death has burst
forth into life, all subduing.
His enemy now vanquished see:
his death has been death's undoing.
"And yours shall be like victory
o'er death and grave," says he, who gave
his life for us, life renewing.

Georg Vetter, tr. Martin H. Franzmann, "With High Delight Let Us Unite"
Text © 1969 Concordia Publishing House

LOVING IS BELIEVING

The Resurrection of Our Lord/Easter Day: John 20:1–18

Naturally, reflection on these verses is often focused on Mary Magdalene. More telling for the journey of faith, though, is John's account of the experience of Peter and the other disciple, the one whom Jesus loved, in the empty tomb.

The other disciple reaches the tomb first but does not enter. Peter goes in and inspects the linen wrappings as evidence indeed that Jesus' body has disappeared. (Because John does not report his reaction we imagine he is merely puzzled. Luke, whose account features Peter only, says Peter went away "marveling at what had happened.")

But the other disciple then entered, "and he saw and believed."

Why did Peter not also see and believe? The answer is: love.

This was the "disciple whom Jesus loved" and he loved Jesus in return. Love opened his eyes to the truth about Jesus and it will do the same for us. Through prayer, meditation, worship, and song, our faith is increased and we grow in our ability to love God and to be a channel for God's love in return flowing out into a world in need.

Lord of eternal life, let love be the song
through which we proclaim the truth of your resurrection.

Lo, Jesus meets thee, risen from the tomb!
Lovingly he greets thee, scatters fear and gloom;
let his church with gladness hymns of triumph sing,
for the Lord now liveth; death has lost its sting!

Edmond Budry, tr. R. Birch Hoyle, "Thine Is the Glory"

STAY WITH US

The Resurrection of Our Lord/Easter Evening: Luke 24:13–49

How close, in Luke's narrative, the touching, heartwarming, life-changing events of Easter evening came to not happening at all!

On the road to Emmaus, discussing the events leading up to Jesus' crucifixion, the two disciples are joined by the risen Savior, whom they do not recognize. At first Jesus patiently listens, then interprets to them "the things about himself in all the scriptures." Still they do not realize who he is.

Yet, something is tugging at them, for they urgently desire to remain with him. As the three approach Emmaus, Jesus moves ahead as if to continue on. "But they urged him strongly, saying, 'Stay with us. …'"

That simple invitation leads to a life-altering, world-changing series of events. The disciples recognize him in the breaking of bread. They rush to Jerusalem to tell the others. Jesus then appears to them all, shares a meal with them and opens them all to a full understanding of the scriptures.

As we make our preparations for worship each Sunday, let us extend that same invitation to our risen Savior: "Stay with us, Lord!" Then we too will experience our hearts burning as the truth of God's Word is opened in the midst of the assembly.

Self-giving God, open our hearts
so that we invite your risen Son into our midst in all we do.

Now I will cling forever to Christ, my Savior true;
my Lord will leave me never, whate'er he passes through.
He rends death's iron chain; he breaks through sin and pain;
he shatters hell's grim thrall; I follow him through all.
Paul Gerhardt, tr. John Kelly, "Awake, My Heart, with Gladness"

BELIEVING IS NOT SEEING

Second Sunday of Easter: John 20:19–31

"Seeing is believing." This could be a headline for John 20, at least up through verse 28. Throughout these verses we are introduced to four types of faith through sight—the Beloved Disciple, viewing the grave-cloths in the empty tomb; Mary Magdalene, seeing the risen Jesus and hearing him call her name; the disciples, rejoicing when they see their risen Lord; and Thomas, ultimately, when Jesus shows him his wounds and invites him to touch them.

But the message of the verse that follows, John 20:29, is that *not* seeing, yet believing, expresses a deeper order of faith. Here we find the Jesus of John's Gospel shifting his attention from the disciples to the audience—to us, the readers down through the ages—as he makes clear that his ultimate concern is for those who have come to believe through the words of Jesus' disciples.

Human nature causes many of us to insist on signs and wonders as a gauge of belief. But we know from Hebrews 11 that faith is "the assurance of things hoped for, the evidence of things not seen." Let the assurance of faith, not the evidence of sight, be the conviction which fills our music-making.

God of infinite love,
ground our faith in absolute trust in your goodness and mercy.

We walk by faith and not by sight;
with gracious words draw near,
O Christ, who spoke as none e'er spoke:
"My peace be with you here."

Henry Alford, "We Walk by Faith"

PERFECT FREEDOM

Third Sunday of Easter: John 21:1–19

At first glance, Jesus' familiar dialogue with Peter upon his third post-resurrection appearance presents an enigma. Why does Jesus keep asking Peter
whether he loves him? Peter is perplexed, and so are we.

Yet the point Jesus is trying to get across is bracingly simple: As a follower
of Christ, obedience is required. We are no longer free to do as we choose.

Martin Luther understood intimately the perils of unbridled freedom of
the will. "Free choice is worst when it is best," he wrote. "What choice has the
will when reason dictates to it only the darkness of its own blind ignorance?"
Instead, Luther goes on to say, we are to look to the voice of the gospel to
reveal Christ.[3]

How compelling that voice is in these verses:

"Tend my lambs."

"Shepherd my sheep."

"Tend my sheep."

And finally: "Follow me!"

As musicians of the church we are both followers (of Christ) and leaders
(of the assembly's song). It is a high and holy calling!

God of grace, let us find perfect freedom in our perfect obedience to you.

"Come, follow me," the Savior spake,
"all in my way abiding:
deny yourselves, the world forsake,
obey my call and guiding."

Johann Scheffler, tr. Charles W. Shaeffer, "Come, Follow Me, the Savior Spake"

SHEPHERD US, O GOD

Fourth Sunday of Easter: John 10:22–30

Earlier in John 10, in conversation with the Pharisees Jesus has spoken of himself as shepherd, gatekeeper, gate, and good shepherd. But not until these verses does he address the sheep.

"If you are the Messiah, tell us plainly," the Pharisees demand, clearly confused by each of Jesus' attempts to explain his identity. "I have told you, and you do not believe," Jesus patiently answers. "The works that I do in my Father's name testify to me; but you do not believe, because you do not belong to my sheep."

But this is not the end of the story, as we know from John 10:16. There, Jesus says, "I have other sheep that do not belong to this fold. I must bring them also, and they will listen to my voice."

One of the driving forces in ministry today is to bring in sheep which do not belong to the fold. Unfortunately, music—and by extension worship—is often appropriated as a tool for evangelism. Musical styles which echo pop culture are imposed onto worship in the hope that the culture-friendly feel will attract new members.

We all have experienced this to some extent. Occasionally it seems to be effective but more often it simply alienates those sheep already in the fold. What other approaches to enlivening our worship are possible that communicate our Savior's voice without sacrificing the substance of his message?

Jesus, our Good Shepherd, fill us with creative vision
so that we may help others follow the sound of your voice.

Gather us in, the lost and forsaken,
gather us in, the blind and the lame;
call to us now, and we shall awaken,
we shall arise at the sound of our name.

Marty Haugen, "Gather Us In"
Text © 1982 GIA Publications, Inc.

GOOD SHEEP

Fifth Sunday of Easter: John 13:31–35

The readings assigned for the fourth and fifth Sundays of Easter may be considered together. Even though they are separated by a few chapters, the second extends and expands the implications of the first in the manner that we so often encounter in the cycle of readings prescribed by the Revised Common Lectionary.

The Fourth Sunday of Easter, April 25 this year, is often referred to as Good Shepherd Sunday. But here in Year C it might better be called "Good Sheep Sunday."

The question in John 10:22–30 is not whether Jesus is the Good Shepherd, but who fits the description of "good sheep." Those who do not believe, Jesus tells us, do not "belong to my sheep." We go on to read in verses 26–28:

My sheep hear my voice. I know them, and they follow me.
I give them eternal life, and they will never perish.
No one will snatch them out of my hand.

This is a capsule description of the contemplative life. We are intimately familiar with the sound of Jesus' voice. We are intimately known and loved by him.

In our busy schedules, do we regularly make time for this relationship? We must, for it is of critical importance to the well-being of the congregation in which we serve and to the life of the world. Just as Jesus loves us, we know from John 13:35, we are to love others. "By this everyone will know that you are my disciples, if you have love for one another."

God of faith, help us to make time each day in which we focus only on you
so that we may grow in your love and bring it to others.

Early let us seek your favor,
early let us do your will;
blessed Lord and only Savior,
with your love our spirits fill.

attr. Dorothy A. Thrupp, "Savior, like a Shepherd Lead Us"

INDWELLING

Sixth Sunday of Easter: John 14:23–29

Verse 27 from this reading is familiar to many: "Peace I leave with you; my peace I give to you. I do not give to you as the world gives. Do not let your hearts be troubled, and do not let them be afraid." But let us instead consider the implications of verse 23:

> *Jesus answered him, 'Those who love me will keep my word, and my Father will love them, and we will come to them and make our home with them.'*

The spiritual life is one of obedience to Jesus' teachings, cultivated through careful study of and interaction with scripture. As we read God's Word, we find that we are imperceptibly and incomprehensibly changed.

The spiritual life is also grounded in the indwelling of the Triune God in each faithful heart. Jesus is neither a concept nor an authority figure; rather, our hearts become his home. This allows us to understand Jesus' response to Thomas' plaintive question back in John 14:5, 'Lord, we do not know where you are going. How can we know the way?"

Jesus answers him with the "what": "I am the way, and the truth, and the life." Here in these verses, however, we discover the "where": straight to the center of our hearts. If we begin each day with this understanding, it will shine like a beacon through all that we do.

God of endless time and space, live in us so that we may be reborn in you.

O Holy Spirit, enter in
and in our hearts your work begin,
and make our hearts your dwelling.
Michael Schirmer, tr. Catherine Winkworth, "O Holy Spirit, Enter In"

MINISTERS OF WORSHIP

The Ascension of Our Lord: Luke 24:44–53

*Then he led them out as far as Bethany, and, lifting up his hands, he blessed them.
While he was blessing them, he withdrew from them and was carried up into heaven.
And they worshipped him, and returned to Jerusalem with great joy;
and they were continually in the temple blessing God. (Luke 24:50–53)*

Faced with declining membership, some mainstream denominations are concentrating their energies and resources in mission and evangelism. Certainly there are scriptural incentives for this, such as at the end of Matthew ("Go therefore and make disciples of all nations…") and here in Luke 24:47 ("repentance and forgiveness of sins is to be proclaimed in [the Messiah's] name to all nations…").

It seems too often, however, that these efforts far overshadow the attention given to worship. Isn't worship what we are first and foremost about as the body of Christ? Let us take this final magnificent image in Luke as our inspiration, in which the disciples are in the temple worshiping Jesus in an attitude of "great joy."

How life-giving it would be if our worship services exhibited this same joy week in and week out. We musicians are ministers of worship, not of mission. Let us embrace Ascension as a time to make that known.

Creating God, let our hands, feet, and lips serve as joyful instruments for the sounding of your praise.

---

*You servants of God, your Master proclaim,
and publish abroad his wonderful name;
the name, all victorious, of Jesus extol;
his kingdom is glorious and rules over all.*

Charles Wesley, "You Servants of God"

BECOMING ONE

Seventh Sunday of Easter: John 17:20–26

Father, I desire that those also, whom you have given me, may be with me where I am… (John 17:24)

As is so often true of the psalms, these verses lift us across barriers of time and space. Jesus' great prayer in John 17 is not only offered on behalf of his disciples, it is offered on our behalf as well.

To become one with Jesus, to be with him and to see his glory, is not a matter of simply shutting our eyes and imagining Christ's peace washing over us. In truth, the path to communion with our Lord and Savior is fraught with struggle. Temptations divert us. Enemies assail us. "We are afflicted in every way, but not crushed; perplexed, but not driven to despair; persecuted, but not forsaken; struck down, but not destroyed," Paul writes in 2 Corinthians 4, "always carrying in the body the death of Jesus so that the life of Jesus may be made visible in our bodies."

The music of our worship services should tell of this ordeal, to some extent. If everything was easy and familiar it wouldn't be authentically Christian. Proclamation cannot reassure. It must challenge and exhort. And we must be well-prepared, fearless leaders in that exhortation.

Lord of heaven and earth, make us courageous ambassadors of your Word.

Since we are all one in the Lord,
as we gather, let us be watchful that no strife still divide us.
Contention, envy, ill will, spite—may these all cease;
with us, abiding in our midst, is Christ our God.

Latin plainsong, 9th century, "Where True Charity and Love Abide"
Text © 1995, 2001 Augsburg Fortress

LOVING JESUS

The Day of Pentecost: John 14:8–17 [25–27]

Taking our cue from the Acts 2 reading, we often approach Pentecost as a day of high drama filled with images of wind, fire, and the cacophony of praise in a multiplicity of languages.

If we concentrate instead on the Gospel reading we are invited to engage in something much more intimate of which the New Testament speaks only rarely—loving Jesus.

How easy this is, and how great the reward. "If you love me, you will keep my commandments. And I will ask the Father, and he will give you another Advocate, to be with you forever" (John 14:15–16).

Perfect love of Jesus means there is nothing we would not do for him. Perfect love is also freeing: No longer must we debate our course of action. We simply do what Jesus commands (John 13:34). And in return Jesus gives us the gift of the Holy Spirit to kindle in the hearts of God's faithful people the fire of the Spirit's love, and to renew the face of the earth.

Let us take every opportunity in our music-making to convey the truth not only of Jesus' love for us but of our capacity to express our perfect love of Jesus.

*Come, Holy Spirit, fill the hearts of your faithful
and kindle in them the fire of your love.
Send forth your Spirit and they shall be created.
And you shall renew the face of the earth.*

*Come, Holy Ghost, God and Lord,
with all your graces now outpoured
on each believer's mind and heart;
your fervent love to them impart.*

Martin Luther, "Come, Holy Ghost, God and Lord"

PROPHETIC WITNESSES

The Holy Trinity (First Sunday after Pentecost): John 16:12–15

"...for he will not speak on his own, but will speak whatever he hears, and he will declare to you the things that are to come." (John 16: 13)

This beautiful description by the Johannine Jesus of the activity of the Holy Spirit can be received in the context of our own ministries. Through our music we serve as prophetic witnesses to "the way of all truth." Writes John scholar Raymond Brown, "the best Christian preparation for what is coming to pass is not an exact foreknowledge of the future but a deep understanding of what Jesus means for one's own time."[4]

Whether we are choir members, organists, instrumentalists, or conductors, we are ministers of God's Word through music. Therefore we first locate our relationship to God in prayer and then ground ourselves prayer in the knowledge of scripture. That enables us to translate our experience of God into sound using the gifts God has given us, in a way that engages the hearts and minds of those in our midst.

God, source of all goodness,
thank you for the gifts and abilities with which you have entrusted us.
Help us to use them for your glory.

Praise, all you people, the name so holy,
the Lord who does such wondrous things!
All that has being, to praise God solely,
with happy heart its amen sings!

Johann D. Herrnschmidt, "Praise the Almighty!"
Text © 2006 Augsburg Fortress

THE TREASURE OF THE HEART, PART II

Proper 3 (Lectionary 8—if observed): Luke 6:29–39

In the church, as in the rest of life, we encounter those who say one thing and do another. Perhaps our pastors or parishioners praise us to our face but work to undermine us behind our backs. But in the church, as in the rest of life, we are called to a higher path, one which involves complete transformation in Christ with utter consistency between the inner and outer person. This is the purpose of Jesus' list of "parables" in this reading.

With them we recall Paul's words in Colossians 3:12–15: "As God's chosen ones, holy and beloved, clothe yourselves with compassion, kindness, humility, meekness, and patience. Bear with one another and, if anyone has a complaint against another, forgive each other; just as the Lord has forgiven you, so you also must forgive. Above all, clothe yourselves with love, which binds everything together in perfect harmony. And let the peace of Christ rule in your hearts, to which indeed you were called in the one body."

And, Paul adds, "be thankful."

We can't control the actions of others but we do have jurisdiction over our own inner and outer lives. Let us concentrate on the "good treasure of the heart" (Luke 6:45) and our ministry will flourish out of that abundance.

God of compassion, lift us out of our selfish ways of thinking and help us to focus instead on our service to you.

Lord, you can help when earthly armor fails us;
Lord, you can save when deadly sin assails us;
and, in the day when hell itself appalls us,
grant us your peace, Lord.

Matthäus von Löwenstern, tr. Philip Pusey, "Lord of Our Life"

FAITH THAT HEALS

Proper 4 (Lectionary 9—if observed): Luke 7:1–10

Luke's account of the Roman soldier with the desperately ill slave presents us with an image of great faith and great humility. Apparently frantic with worry over his beloved slave, the centurion instructs local leaders to find Jesus, whose prophetic words (Luke 6) had undoubtedly caused a great stir, and bring him to the slave's bedside so that he might be healed.

The message is duly delivered and Jesus is on his way, but in the meantime the centurion is overcome by his own unworthiness and sends another message: "Do not trouble yourself, for I am not worthy to have you come under my roof." Yet, his faith does not collapse in the midst of this personal crisis. Quite the contrary in fact, for he recognizes that Jesus' divinity and power exceed mere geography. "But only speak the word," he says through his messengers, "and let my servant be healed."

Deeply touched, Jesus turns to the crowd: "I tell you, not even in Israel have I found such faith."

When we find our sense of worthiness in God's sight shaken to the core, let us embrace our faith ever more deeply—"the assurance of things hoped for, the conviction of things not seen" (Hebrews 11)—and allow that confidence to flow out through our music.

Almighty God, strengthen our faith
so that we may become agents of Christ's healing power.

No storm can shake my inmost calm while to that Rock I'm clinging.
Since Christ is Lord of heaven and earth, how can I keep from singing?

Robert Lowry, "How Can I Keep from Singing?"

JESUS IS LORD

Proper 5 (Lectionary 10): Luke 7:11–17

Jesus' raising of the widow's son at Nain is an excellent reading to follow the Sunday after Holy Trinity because it testifies to Jesus not simply as prophet but as Lord.

The story recalls that in 1 Kings 17 of Elijah and the widow of Zarephath. There, as the widow's son lay lifeless, Elijah vigorously pleads with the Lord to restore him. Here in Luke, however, Jesus speaks directly to the dead boy: "Young man, I say to you, rise!"

"A great prophet has risen among us!" the crowds exclaim. Yet neither they nor the disciples grasp that Jesus is Lord. How persuasively do we testify through our music to this central truth that it is he to whom every knee shall bow? Jesus is not merely a teacher, nor a healer, nor a companion nor a friend: Jesus is Lord!

> **Triune God, fix our eyes on God the Son**
> **as the pioneer and perfecter of our faith.**

> *In your hearts enthrone him; there let him subdue*
> *all that is not holy, all that is not true.*
> *Crown him as your captain in temptation's hour;*
> *let his will enfold you in its light and pow'r.*

Caroline M. Noel, "At the Name of Jesus"

FORGIVENESS AND GRACE

Proper 6 (Lectionary 11): Luke 7:36–8:3

"…her sins, which are many, have been forgiven, for she loved much; but he who is forgiven little, loves little." (Luke 7:47)

It usually takes a big transgression for us to beg God for forgiveness. Receiving it, we experience overwhelming gratitude for God's mercy. We do not deserve to be taken back into God's loving arms and yet this is what God always does. This is grace.

We don't know exactly what kind of sinful life the woman with the alabaster jar had been leading. Clearly though, with Jesus she had experienced forgiveness. Her response was expressed in acts of love—as she wept, she bathed his feet with her tears, lovingly dried them with her hair, then kissed and anointed his feet with ointment.

What about all the little transgressions we commit—the unkind word, the thoughtless gesture, the missed opportunities to minister to those in need? Shouldn't we beg God for forgiveness for those as well as for our bigger acts of defiance? In that case we would experience grace as virtually a constant condition, since our string of sins seems to be never-ending. Let that outpouring of gratitude be the substance of our song.

> *God of boundless grace, thank you for loving us*
> *no matter how, when, or why we turn away from you.*
> *Thank you for taking us back into your arms.*

There's a wideness in God's mercy, like the wideness of the sea;
there's a kindness in God's justice which is more than liberty.
There is no place where earth's sorrows are more felt than up in heav'n.
There is no place where earth's failings have such kindly judgment giv'n.

Frederick W. Faber, "There's a Wideness in God's Mercy"

CROSSING OVER

Proper 7 (Lectionary 12): Luke 8:26–39

The story of the so-called "Gerasene demoniac" is all about reaching across boundaries of acceptability to do ministry. Jesus has just crossed the sea of Galilee in a frightful storm. Stepping out of the boat, he is accosted by a wild man who is the very picture of ritual uncleanliness: The man goes without clothes, lives in tombs and on top of that is possessed by a legion of demons.

Undeterred (of course), Jesus commands the demons to come out of the man. As an exclamation point to the *cantus firmus* of uncleanliness, the demons rush out of the man into a herd of swine.

Instead of reading this as just another healing story, perhaps we can see it as one of proclamation across nearly insurmountable boundaries. What Jewish rabbi, for example, would minister to such a person under these conditions?

Let us put ourselves in Jesus' shoes and imagine what this scenario might look like in our own context. How, through music, could we minister to those on the margins with whom we might not otherwise be able to engage in spiritual dialogue? And how might these efforts yield new sources of strength for our ministry?

> **God of justice, give us the courage to preach the Gospel**
> **in places where we would otherwise never dare to go.**

Praise the One who breaks the darkness with a liberating light;
praise the One who frees the pris'ners, turning blindness into sight.
Praise the One who preached the gospel, healing ev'ry dead disease,
calming storms and feeding thousands with the very bread of peace.

Rusty Edwards, "Praise the One Who Breaks the Darkness"
Text © 1987 Hope Publishing Company

DON'T LOOK BACK

Proper 8 (Lectionary 13): Luke 9:51–62

"I came to bring fire to the earth, and how I wish it were already kindled!" Jesus says in Luke 12:49. It is one of the most startling verses in all the Gospels.

Such is the reality of Jesus' ministry. It's a far cry from the kindly image of the good shepherd that is displayed on posters, portraits and pendants throughout the typical Christian bookstore.

As we see in this week's reading, the life of the true disciple of Jesus is similarly turbulent. Journeying to Jerusalem, Jesus is approached by two "would-be" followers. For both, however, the decision to come with Jesus is conditional. One asks permission to first bury his father and the other to bid farewell to his family.

What kindly teacher would refuse potential students the dignity of such acts of familial compassion?

Jesus does not deny their request outright. Instead, by means of a terse image, he articulates the urgent need for absolute unity of purpose in the life of the disciple: "No one who puts a hand to the plow and looks back is fit for the kingdom of God."

In how many ways do we accommodate the call to follow Jesus to our own convenience? "I could go and help feed the homeless, but I really need that time to practice." "I would invite a stranger in, but that might make my family uncomfortable."

When we are so fully filled with the Spirit that we *are* able to put our hand to the plow and focus only on the kingdom of God, imagine how glorious that sight will be!

Eternal God, give us singleness of purpose in our desire to follow you.

––––––––––––––––––––

*Give me the strength to do with ready heart and willing
whatever you command, my calling here fulfilling…*
Johann Heermann, tr. Catherine Winkworth, "O God, My Faithful God"

LIKE A FLASH OF LIGHTNING

Proper 9 (Lectionary 14): Luke 10:1–11, 16–20

The omission from the Revised Common Lectionary of verses 12–15, in which Jesus chastises Chorazin, Bethsaida, and Capernaum for having rejected him, diminishes the powerful articulation of mission in this lesson.

As expressed through this account of the commissioning of the seventy, working to bring in the harvest is not simply a matter of cheerfully spreading the good news. It is doing battle with the Satan. Further, this conflict is not transitory but is instead eschatological, grounded in the victory of life over death. We understand this in verse 18 after the seventy disciples return in triumph. Jesus affirms their authority over the devil's dark forces: "I watched Satan fall from heaven like a flash of lightning."

We dare not take *our* sense of mission too lightly. Dark forces continue to churn beneath the sugar-coated spirituality of pop culture. Do we have the courage to break through that shell and confront these head-on? Music is a powerful means of leading others into this eschatological struggle. We engage it on behalf of God's kingdom not to prove that "the spirits submit" to us (verse 20) but so that our "names are written in heaven."

God of heaven and earth, help us open the gates of your kingdom using the glorious gift of music with which you have entrusted us.

Lead on, O King eternal: we follow, not with fears,
for gladness breaks like morning where'er your face appears.
Your cross is lifted o'er us; we journey in its light;
the crown awaits the conquest; lead on, O God of might!

Ernest W. Shurtleff, "Lead On, O King Eternal"

DOING LIKEWISE

Proper 10 (Lectionary 15): Luke 10:25–37

"Go and do likewise." This in a nutshell is what the parable of the Good Samaritan is all about—*doing*. We attest to the kingdom of God not because of who we say we are or what we say we believe, but because of what we do.

Consider the subject in this tale. On the surface he is completely the wrong person for the job. For one thing, he's a Samaritan and is regarded as an outcast in the region around Jerusalem. For another, he's not even an official man of God, unlike the priest and the Levite.

But the Samaritan's actions are consistent with Jesus' teachings while those of the official men of God are not.

"What must I *do* to inherit eternal life?" the lawyer asks Jesus at the outset of this reading. "Go and *do* likewise," Jesus tells him at the end. As servants of God and the church it is not enough that we perform our prescribed duties efficiently. Our ministry must also be one of compassionate action.

What acts of mercy define our typical week? We work hard to get things together for each worship service. But in the midst of all that we must be attentive to those circumstances that call us to compassionate action. The lives of others, and our own as well, depend on it.

God of compassion, keep us mindful amid the bustle of our weekly activities that we are the hands, feet and eyes of Christ.

---

*Christ in me, and I am freed for living
and forgiving, heart of flesh for lifeless stone;
now bold to serve him, now cheered his love to own,
nevermore alone.*

Tranoscius, 1636; tr. Jaroslav J. Vajda, "God, My Lord, My Strength"
Text © 1969 Concordia Publishing House

RIGHT RELATIONSHIP

Proper 11 (Lectionary 16): Luke 10:38–42

The beautiful cameo of Mary and Martha emerges as a crescendo in the refrain of hospitality sounded throughout Luke 9 and 10. Embracing a small child in Luke 9:48, Jesus tells the disciples, "Whoever welcomes this child in my name welcomes me, and whoever welcomes me welcomes the one who sent me." In Luke 10:16 he pronounces to the crowd of disciples, "...whoever rejects you rejects me, and whoever rejects me rejects the one who sent me."

We are to welcome our Lord with our whole heart, using music as a gateway to that invitation. How often do we allow our intimate connection with God to be disrupted by anxiety about what we think we "should" be doing, as did Martha? Our manufactured expectations ("I know he'd like it if...") become like little idols. We worship them at the expense of the true Lord. If and when we free ourselves from their grip, we discover God is absent. Did Martha grasp Jesus' gentle admonition in verses 41 and 42 at the time or only after he left?

*God of grace, calm our anxieties and strengthen our faith
so that we may joyfully remain in your presence all our days.*

*How oft in making music, we have found
a new dimension in the world of sound,
as worship moved us to a more profound
Alleluia!*

Fred Pratt Green, "When in Our Music God Is Glorified"
Text © 1972 Hope Publishing Company

PERSEVERANCE AND PRAYER

Proper 12 (Lectionary 17): Luke 11:1–13

"For everyone who asks receives, and everyone who searches finds, and for everyone who knocks, the door will be opened." (Luke 11:10)

This familiar verse is not telling us that we'll get whatever we want. Note that it is set up by Luke's version of the Lord's Prayer in verses 2–4. This juxtaposition makes the point that whatever we ask *in Christ's name* (John 14:13–14) will be given us. As faithful Christians we do not invoke the Lord's name in vain: Our petitions in Christ's name come from depths of our hearts, and God hears them.

The context for Luke 11:10 is not just faith but also perseverance. How easily we may become discouraged when our hymn suggestions are overruled, when choir members skip rehearsals without letting us know, when a bell choir member suddenly quits in the middle of the year, or when our copious preparations week after week seem to fall on deaf ears.

Instead of seeking affirmation from the world, Jesus exhorts us to go to God in prayer. "How much more will the heavenly Father give the Holy Spirit to those who ask him!"

God of the cosmos,
fill us with the knowledge that you are always waiting with open arms
to receive our petitions in your Son's name.

━━━━━━━━━━━━━

You are the way; through You alone
can we the Father find;
in you, O Christ, has God revealed
his heart and will and mind.

George W. Doane, "You Are the Way"

FREE TO LOVE

Proper 13 (Lectionary 18): Luke 12:13–21

Here we come face to face with the rich man who gloats over the prospect of ever-larger storehouses for his wealth, only to find his life is being demanded of him that very night. What does this tell us about our own attachments and the barriers they erect between us and God?

The rich man's addiction to things kept him from seeing how his life and wealth might have been used for the kingdom of God. Most of us probably don't have large storehouses of wealth to worry about. What about our attachment to certain worship practices? Are we so stuck in our allegiance to certain worship styles that we aren't able to consider how our gifts might be used in other ways to open minds and hearts to God's presence?

To see this in another way, begin at the heart of the worship experience. How can thanksgiving, adoration, confession, and praise be most powerfully sung so that God's love is returned to us in greater measure? What faith-filled forms of worship might that exchange assume?

> *God of creation, free us from our attachments to things*
> *so that we may always make our beginning in you.*

Watch against the devil's snares
Lest asleep he find you.
For indeed no pains he spares
to deceive and blind you.
Satan's prey
oft are they
who secure are sleeping
and no watch are keeping.

Johann Burkhard Freystein, tr. Catherine Winkworth, "Rise, My Soul, to Watch and Pray"

GOD BETWEEN THE NOTES

Proper 14 (Lectionary 19): Luke 12:32–40

Watchfulness is the key word in this passage from Luke.

Not just casual watchfulness, though, as if we are lazily scanning the horizon, but that of high alert and acute anticipation. We are to "be like the slaves who are waiting for their master to return from the wedding banquet so that they may open the door for him *as soon as* he comes and knocks" (Luke 12:36). The servants are so eager for their master's return that they are positioned just inside the door, straining for the slightest aural indication of his impending arrival and ready to fling wide the door to welcome him in.

How can we translate this into music?

It doesn't mean playing fast and loud. Rather, this passage from Luke invites us to discover a way of making music in which each note matters. In this state of heightened alert we pay attention to every step of the journey and are particularly attuned to the way in which one note leads to the next. We come to understand that it is *between* the notes that God's presence is conveyed and meaning is found.

God of infinite creativity,
increase our awareness of music's expressive possibilities
so that through them we may convey your truth.

Our hope and expectation,
O Jesus, now appear;
arise, O Sun so longed for,
o'er this benighted sphere.
With hearts and hands uplifted,
we plead, O Lord, to see
the day of earth's redemption
That sets your people free.

Laurentius Laurenti, tr. Sarah B. Findlater, "Rejoice, Rejoice, Believers"

PEACE—OR DIVISION?

Proper 15 (Lectionary 20): Luke 12:49–56

In this week's passage we experience these jarring words of Jesus: "Do you think I have come to bring peace to the earth? No, I tell you, but rather division!" How do we reconcile with the angels' song on the night of Jesus' birth: "Glory to God in the highest heaven, and on earth, peace among those with whom God is pleased!" (Luke 2:14)

Which is it…peace or division?

In Luke 2 the angels herald Jesus' birth for its ultimate meaning. That event sets in motion the reign of God on earth, leading to Jesus' crucifixion and resurrection in which all creation is redeemed. Here in Luke 12 we are dealing not with redemption but with the nature of Jesus' ministry, then as well as now. As Joel Green puts it, "As Luke has continually shown, and as Jesus has endeavored to teach his followers, the realization of God's purpose will engender opposition from those who serve a contrary aim."[5]

This tells us that we should expect opposition in the course of our own ministries as we proclaim the good news. Do we find resistance to those worship practices that we believe best mediate an encounter with the risen Christ? Do jealous co-workers attempt to undermine us? Do our best efforts go unnoticed?

What we can do is use each of these experiences as invitations for self-examination. Are there ways we could be still more effective? And what do these experiences tell us about the location of our ministry in God's time? "You know how to interpret the appearance of earth and sky," Jesus says accusingly to the crowds, "but why do you not know how to interpret the present time?"

Eternal God, equip us for ministry
so that we may not be discouraged by opposition
but find in all our encounters new sources of strength in you.

───────────────

But if, forgetful, we should find your yoke is hard to bear;
if worldly pressures fray the mind and love itself cannot unwind
its tangled skein of care: our inward life repair.

Fred Pratt Green, "How Clear Is Our Vocation, Lord"
Text © 1982 Hope Publishing Company

HEALED AND FREED

Proper 16 (Lectionary 21): Luke 13:10–17

Luke's account of Jesus' healing of the crippled woman is short on detail. Recalling the more dramatic description of Jesus' healing of the hemorrhaging woman in Luke 8, we are left wondering what this afflicted woman's response was to being summoned by him. Did she have any idea who he was or what lay in store for her when she drew nearer?

Nonetheless the result is the same as in the earlier story: The woman encounters Jesus directly. She is healed and is immediately filled with the desire to praise God.

This is what happens to us when we recognize our afflictions (pride, envy, greed, sloth) and hear Jesus' voice calling us. We draw near and are healed. How can our music become the voice which calls people into Christ's presence so that they, too, may be freed from spirits that have kept them crippled?

*God of hope, give us the courage to face the dark spirits
that keep us in chains, and come to you for healing.*

---

*How clear is our vocation, Lord, when once we heed your call
to live according to your word and daily learn, refreshed, restored,
that you are Lord of all
and will not let us fall.*

Fred Pratt Green, "How Clear Is Our Vocation, Lord"
Text © 1982 Hope Publishing Company

RADICAL HOSPITALITY

Proper 17 (Lectionary 22): Luke 14:1, 7–14

Although verses 12–14 precede the parable of the great banquet, they are not about mere hospitality. Instead they the inauguration of a new world order.

In the ancient Mediterranean world, the making and receiving of a dinner invitation was an intricate process. People were seated according to their social status. Higher positions at the table served to enhance the guest's prestige. As well, guests were expected to reciprocate in kind.

The poor would never be invited to such a gathering. Not only did they have no social status, they would be unable to return the favor. Yet Jesus tells the Pharisee dinner host he is to invite them anyway and expect no repayment, "for you will be repaid at the resurrection of the righteous."

What does this great banquet look like for us? We are to let go of the expectation that our acts of hospitality will be rewarded in worldly ways. How freeing that becomes! We can then engage in radical generosity and "random acts of kindness" without anxiety over whether the recipient can return the favor. "The body of Christ, given for you; the blood of Christ, shed for you." Let this be the substance of our song.

God of abundance, fill our hearts with your radical hospitality
so that we may grow into the fullness of your love.

Take my love; my Lord, I pour
at thy feet its treasure store;
take myself, and I will be
ever, only, all for thee.

Francis R. Havergal, "Take My Life, That I May Be"

GOSPEL TRUTH

Proper 18 (Lectionary 23): Luke 14:25–33

For several weeks now we have encountered in Luke some challenging prescriptions for how a Christian should live. We have been meeting Jesus at his counter-cultural best.

In this week's reading he demands that we give up our most cherished worldly attachments. "Whoever comes to me and does not hate father and mother, wife and children, brothers and sisters, yes, and even life itself, cannot be my disciple."

How can we possibly attain this?

We find the answer in his very next sentence: "Whoever does not carry the cross and follow me cannot be my disciple."

Carrying the cross means loving Jesus our Lord with all our heart, mind and soul. We carry the glory of the cross before our eyes, in such a way that we see everything else through it and behind it. In so doing we find that in the course of our lives we "are treated as imposters, and yet are true; as unknown, yet are well known; as dying, and see—we are alive; as punished, yet not killed; as sorrowful, yet always rejoicing; as poor, yet making many rich; has having nothing, yet possessing everything" (2 Corinthians 6:8–10).

We live from the perspective of one sentenced to death whose life as been redeemed. Let us take every opportunity to sing hymns whose texts invite us into this Gospel truth.

Redeeming God, fix our eyes on the cross as the center of our lives.

Then let us follow Christ, our Lord,
and take the cross appointed,
and, firmly clinging to his word,
in suff'ring be undaunted.

Johann Scheffler, tr. Charles W. Shaeffer, "Come Follow Me, the Savior Spake"

LOCATING THE LOST

Proper 19 (Lectionary 24): Luke 15:1–10

Here we encounter the first of Luke's three lost-and-found stories in Chapter 15. It's too bad we don't get them successively in the Revised Common Lectionary (the second and third are assigned to Year C's fourth Sunday of Lent), because the message of God's joy in recovering what was once lost emerges as a powerful crescendo as we move from one story to the next—from the lost sheep to the lost coin and finally to the lost son. Plus, experiencing these in sequence drives home the point that the parable of the prodigal son is *not* about redemption but of recovery of that which was lost.

The sequence is set up by Luke 15:2, "And the Pharisees and the scribes were grumbling and saying, 'This fellow welcomes sinners and eats with them.'" Many of our congregations may pride themselves on strengthening faith through good music and solid preaching. But how much effort do we expend reaching out to those on the fringes of society who hunger for words of confidence and hope?

The sad thing is that, in most congregations, giving to missions is sharply down. Instead, that money is being spent to sustain the status quo within the church.

How can we musicians of the church encourage people to look outward? What might be the result? "Rejoice, for we have found that which was lost!"

God of new beginnings, help us to see every day as a new beginning in you.

Evermore
from thy store
newborn worlds rise and adore.

Joachim Neander, para. Robert Bridges, "All My Hope on God Is Founded"

GOD AND MAMMON

Proper 20 (Lectionary 25): Luke 16:1–13

On the surface the parable of the "dishonest manager" seems to promote poor stewardship. This fellow had already been caught misusing his master's wealth and was about to be fired. Here he does so once again by willfully reducing the amount owed his master by his debtors.

Yet the point is not how the dishonest wealth was acquired, but that the manager astutely used it for the benefit of God's kingdom. By reducing various debts he quickly acquired friends who were willing to care for him as soon as he became jobless. This garners him praise from his master for having acted faithfully—for using the assets of another for the purposes of God's kingdom. In this he demonstrates that his true master is God: "No slave can serve two masters....you cannot serve God and wealth" (mammon).

Consider that, within every Christian congregation, God is our master. However we have acquired our assets (probably not illegally), are we making faithful use of them to strengthen community and build bridges for eternity? Or are we slaves to our bottom line? If it is the latter—that is, if we are jealously guarding our assets—what reason do we have to think God would entrust us with true riches—those of the kingdom of heaven?

*God of the poor, free us from our attachment to things of the world
so that we may use all that you have given us for your glory.*

*"Let none the gospel gift impede;
I make you free; be free indeed!
This final word I leave you."*

Martin Luther, "Dear Christians, One and All, Rejoice"

HUMILITY OR TORMENT?

Proper 21 (Lectionary 26): Luke 16:19–31

To understand why Luke includes the story of Lazarus and the rich man at just this point in his gospel, we really need verses 14–15, omitted from the Revised Common Lectionary, to help make the connection with verse 13: "You cannot serve God and wealth."

We then go on to read in those two verses, "The Pharisees, who were lovers of money, heard all this, and they ridiculed him." Jesus rebukes them: "You are those who justify yourselves in the sight of others; but God knows your hearts; for what is prized by human beings is an abomination in the sight of God."

That leads Jesus to tell this parable about the dangers of extreme selfishness. Its most shocking aspect is not the reversal of roles, with the rich man tormented for eternity while Lazarus rests safely with Abraham, but the rich man's utter lack of humility even at that point. Not only does he beg Abraham for mercy as if it that was his due; he also clings to his worldly attitude of privilege by asking that Lazarus be sent to serve *him* ("send Lazarus to dip the tip of his finger in water and cool my tongue").

We are all guilty of acts of selfishness. When these are exposed, God in God's infinite mercy invites us—begs us—to become humble. Otherwise we *will* endure the fire of torment—perhaps not in the "next life" but certainly in this one.

God of humility, we thank you for the mercy you shower upon us.
Give us a contrite heart
so that we may know the amazing grace of your infinite love.

Lord, let at last thine angels come,
to Abr'ham's bosom bear me more
that I may die unfearing.

Martin Schalling, tr. Catherine Winkworth, "Lord, Thee I Love with All My Heart"

FREE AT THE FOOT OF THE CROSS

Proper 22 (Lectionary 27): Luke 17:5–10

Our culture trains us to expect praise for everything we do, particularly in those situations in which our endurance was tested. Perhaps we must suffer the nagging of a co-worker: "I got through the entire day without once losing my temper. I should get some kind of reward." Or we must put up with a critical mother-in-law: "I held my tongue the entire time, I really deserve something for that." Or we work long hours at our job: "They could never pay me enough for all I do."

Jesus calls us to love our enemies, to do good for those who hate us, and to pray for those who abuse us. This is merely what is expected of us. These acts gain us no material reward. "So you also, when you have done all that you were ordered to do, say, 'We are worthless slaves; we have done only what we ought to have done!'" We hear Micah 6:8 echoing in the background: "He has told you, O mortal, what is good; and what does the Lord require of you but to do justice, to love kindness, and to walk humbly with your God?"

Doing things simply because God expects us to frees us to be fully present at the foot of the cross. We are neither looking ahead to our material reward, nor back to the deed about which we are gloating. How can that blessed freedom find poetic expression in our music?

> *Lord of the harvest, you entrust us with blessings*
> *for which we can never thank you fully.*
> *Fill us with the fervor of compassionate service to others*
> *so that we may meet your Son at the foot of the cross in all that we do.*

> *Unseal our lips to sing your praise*
> *in endless hymns through all our days;*
> *increase our faith and light our minds;*
> *and set us free from doubt that binds.*

Attr. Wilhelm II, tr. Catherine Winkworth, "Lord Jesus Christ, Be Present Now"

GREAT FAITH

Proper 23 (Lectionary 28): Luke 17:11–19

Here in the tale of the ten lepers, Luke continues the theme of startling reversal encountered in the parable of the rich man and Lazarus.

The central character in this story is both a Samaritan *and* a leper—which makes him to Jewish eyes not only an outcast by virtue of ethnic and religious orientation but also one who has been cursed by God. Yet it is such a person as this that Jesus lifts up before the disciples, as an example of one who recognizes God at work and lavishly praises God for his healing.

Remarkable here is not just the man's outpouring of thanksgiving but the fact that he "saw that he was healed." This allows him to grasp that this healing was a divine act. (We do not know for sure that the others even realized they had been cured, since at the time they were still on their way to the temple as Jesus instructed them, where they presumed their cleansing would be performed.)

If we look around we may notice similar expressions of great faith in places where we might least expect them. Let our faith be strengthened by their example.

*God of surprises, nurture and strengthen our faith
through the example of your humble servants
so that we may sing boldly of all that you have done.*

———————————————

*Praise to the Lord, who will prosper your work and defend you;
surely his goodness and mercy shall daily attend you.
Ponder anew what the Almighty can do,
if with his love he befriend you.*

Joachim Neander, tr. Catherine Winkworth, "Praise to the Lord, the Almighty"

LIVING INTO THE ESCHATON

Proper 24 (Lectionary 29): Luke 18:1–8

In our culture of instant gratification, we are often easily discouraged when we do not get what we ask for, either from God or from those around us. Let us take the widow's unrelenting cries for justice as encouragement to persevere in our own appeals to God, through music and in other forms of activism and service, for what we know to be right.

In the parable, the unjust judge finally relented and meted out justice to the poor widow. So how much more swiftly will God respond to our appeals! "And will not God grant justice to his chosen ones to cry to him day and night? Will he delay long in helping them?" (Luke 18:7)

In point of fact, the cry for justice is not discretionary. It is an indispensable part of our calling.

The key is found in verse 1 of this passage: We are to pray and not lose heart. In so doing we are living into the eschaton, a recurring theme in Luke. We ground our lives in the reality of God's kingdom on earth and gauge our every action according to the victory of life over death accomplished in Christ's resurrection. In this way our lives offer a vigorous response to Jesus' question in Luke 18:8: "And yet, when the Son of Man comes, will he find faith on the earth?"

God of justice, increase our faith
so that we may persevere in our cries for justice.

———————————

For the Lord our God shall come
and shall take his harvest home;
from his field shall in that day
all offenses purge away.

Henry Alford, "Come, Ye Thankful People, Come"

FREED TO LOVE

Proper 25, Lectionary 30): Luke 18:9–14

Here we encounter another delightful reversal of expectation. The pious Pharisee goes home unjustified while the thieving toll collector finds favor with God.

What matters is not outward appearances but inward attitude. The world may perceive us in a certain way, but how do we present ourselves before God?

The Pharisee, notably standing alone, boasts of his piety and exalts himself ("God, I thank you that I am not like other people: thieves, rogues, adulterers, or even like this tax collector") while the toll collector beats his breast in remorse ("God, be merciful to me, a sinner!").

This is a touching parable precisely because we can so closely identify with both these characters.

We are all Pharisees in one way or another. The world teaches us to be smug and self-satisfied, and to look down on those of inferior accomplishments. But in truth, we are all sinners.

This parable takes us into the heart of the central theme of Luke, expressed clearly in the setup to the parable of the good Samaritan (Luke 10:25): What must we do to inherit eternal life?

The answer is simple. We are to be like this toll collector in every waking moment: "God, be merciful to me, a sinner!" In so doing we confess our absolute dependence on and trust in our Lord and Savior, which frees us to "love the Lord your God with all your heart, and with all your soul, and with all your strength, and with all your mind; and your neighbor as yourself." (Luke 10:27).

God of mercy, free us from the bondage of fear
so that we may confess our sin before you
and experience the grace of your forgiveness.

Mortal pride and earthly glory,
sword and crown betray our trust;
what with care and toil we fashion,
tow'r and temple, fall to dust.
But thy pow'r, hour by hour,
is my temple and my tow'r.

Joachim Neander, para. Robert Bridges, "All My Hope on God Is Founded"

JOYOUS SAINTS

All Saints Day,
if observed in place of Proper 26/Lectionary 31: Luke 6:20–31

"Conventional wisdom." The term was popularized by John Kenneth Galbraith half a century ago to describe ideas that, although unproven, are familiar, predictable, and therefore accepted by the general public.

How that concept is turned on its head in Luke! The poor, not the rich, will inherit God's kingdom. The hungry will be filled. The grieving will laugh. Those who are excluded, reviled, and defamed will leap for joy.

Jesus is not just speaking in terms of the end times. A new world order has been proclaimed and everything has changed. We are released from the chains of fear and death and are free to embrace the love of God as the ground and essence of our every interaction with the world and those in it. This is what defines the lives of saints—and what makes it possible for each of us to live exactly as they did, whether we are feeding hungry masses in starving nations or simply tending to the needs of those in our home, choir, or church family.

God of hope, teach us to be ambassadors of your love in all that we do.

The world is bright with the joyous saints
who love to do Jesus' will.

Lesbia Scott, "I Sing a Song of the Saints of God"

I'M GOING TO YOUR HOUSE TODAY

Proper 26 (Lectionary 31): Luke 19:1–10

In the tale of Zacchaeus, Jericho's chief tax collector, we find a charming account of discipleship addressed by a favorite Sunday School song. But the song omits one crucial character: the crowd.

It is the crowd, not Zacchaeus' short stature, which obscures his view. The crowd refuses to part to let him through so he may view Jesus passing by.

And when Jesus singles out Zacchaeus, people are incensed at the idea that Jesus would choose to stay with someone whose wealth was ill-gotten: "All who saw it began to grumble." They are prideful and jealous.

But Zacchaeus was focused all along on seeing Jesus. Even the crush of the crowd did not discourage him and he came up with a creative solution (the sycamore tree). The result? He and Jesus met face to face and he was changed. "Look, half of my possessions, Lord, I will give to the poor; and if I have defrauded anyone of anything, I will pay them back *four times* as much."

Do we demonstrate this same determination to see Jesus in our midst? How resourceful can we be when obstacles present themselves? In what ways can music help others overcome those obstacles?

God of wisdom, position us to see your Son face to face in all that we do
so that our hearts may be changed
and our lives become focused on service to you.

Ubi caritas et amor,
Deus ibi est.
(Where charity and love abide,
God is dwelling there.)

Latin antiphon, 9th century

TRUTH AND CONSEQUENCE

Proper 27 (Lectionary 32): Luke 20:27–38

Here the Jewish elders persist in their attempts to trap Jesus "by what he said, so as to hand him over to the jurisdiction and authority of the governor" (v. 20). The Sadducees' convoluted question about whose wife the woman will be in the resurrection, having previously married all seven brothers, is quickly revealed as folly when Luke tells us in an aside that that they don't even believe in resurrection.

Of course Jesus will have none of it. His response emphasizes that interpretation, not blind obedience, is key to understanding Mosaic law, and that eschatological perspective—the ability to see all things from the viewpoint of the resurrection, the final event in history—is in turn the key to interpretation.

How do we interpret the events of our lives? Do we become mired in petty details or are we able, like Jesus, to adopt an eschatological perspective? If we approach scripture and indeed all of life from the embrace of God's victory over death, which *we* know to be true, then all may be understood in the light. For every human action we experience or hear about, we may ask: Does this testify to the triumph of life over death that was accomplished in the resurrection of God's Son?

In this way we will learn to evaluate which signs and powers are of God, and which are not. See 2 Thessalonians 2:8–10, especially:

And then the lawless one will be revealed…in the working of Satan, who uses all power, signs, lying wonders, and every kind of wicked deception for those who are perishing, because they refused to love the truth and so be saved. (2 Thessalonians 2:8–10)

> *Life-giving God, preserve us with your mighty power,*
> *that we may expose the deeds of darkness*
> *in our midst so that truth may be better known among all people.*

Christ is risen! Henceforth never death or hell shall us enthrall.
We are in Christ's, in him forever we have triumphed over all.

John S. B. Monsell, "Christ Is Risen! Alleluia"

AN OPPORTUNITY TO TESTIFY

Proper 28 (Lectionary 33): Luke 21:5–19

Nation will rise against nation, and kingdom against kingdom; there will be great earthquakes, and in various places famines and plagues; and there will be dreadful portents and great signs from heaven. But before all this occurs, they will arrest you and persecute you; they will hand you over to synagogues and prisons, and you will be brought before kings and governors because of my name. (Luke 21:10–12)

Many of us who have led relatively quiet lives may find it hard to relate to these verses. What does this apocalyptic-sounding scenario have to do with us? What do we know of famines, plagues and dreadful portents?

Persecution, though, might sound more familiar. Perhaps co-workers or people in the congregation are on a mission to undermine us in various ways. Perhaps they are even trying to get rid of us. Or maybe you've already received your pink slip after years of faithful service, with not even a severance package as is customary in the professional workplace.

What is your response?

This will give you an opportunity to testify.

No matter what befalls us, Jesus tells us that are to use it to affirm the victory of life over death. We do not return evil for evil but instead proclaim the Gospel in response. The future of the world depends on it.

***Lord of heaven and earth, we thank you for the outpouring of blessings
with which you have graced our lives.
Make us worthy stewards of all these gifts
so that we may shine the light of our Son
into the darkest corners of our world.***

---

*In deepest night, in darkest days,
when harps are hung, no songs we raise,
when silence must suffice as praise,
yet sounding in us quietly there is the song of God.*

Susan Palo Cherwien, "In Deepest Night"
Text © 1995 Susan Palo Cherwien, admin. Augsburg Fortress

HOPE

Christ the King, Proper 29 (Lectionary 34): Luke 23:33–43

It is always a great gift to be in the Gospel of Luke at Christ the King Sunday[6] because this reading embodies the essence of Christ's kingship more perfectly than that for Year A of the Revised Common Lectionary (the judgment day at which the Son of Man separates the sheep from the goats in Matthew 25:31–46) and Year B (Jesus' discourse with Pilate over the nature of his kingship in John 18:33–37).

Throughout Year C, in what amounted to a yearlong Lenten journey, we trudged the dusty roads with the outcast, the despised, the poor, the sick, the lost, the needy. We wept in sorrow as they confessed their brokenness and shed tears of joy as they were gathered into Jesus' healing arms. Along the way we discovered that we, too, are lost and desperately in need of a Savior.

Then, here at the culmination of the church year, we are met with the ultimate expression of Christ's kingship: "Father, forgive them," Jesus prays from the cross, "for they do not know what they are doing."

The prayer recalls the exhortation from Luke 6 which we heard on All Saints Sunday to "pray for those who abuse you." It embodies not only forgiveness but also compassion, fitting for one whose kingship consists not of authority and domination but of humility and service.

For many of us this is the Gospels' hardest lesson to learn. Yet, if we can stand beside Jesus on the cross just as we walked the road with the bent-over woman, the grateful leper, the blind beggar and all those in Jesus' parables, we will discover in ourselves vast reservoirs of compassion and love that we never knew were there. And we will find, step by step, that our faith is increased.

God of majesty, strengthen our hope
so that your love may be poured into our hearts
through the Holy Spirit which has been given to us. Amen.

Though some would make their greatness felt
and lord it over all,
you said the first must be the last
and service be our call.

Delores Dufner, "O Christ, What Can It Mean for Us"
Text © 2001, 2003 GIA Publications, Inc.

NOTES

1. Joel Brown, *The Gospel of Luke*, 170-171.

2. Raymond Brown, *The Gospel According to John I-XII*, 109.

3. "On the Bondage of the Will," in Timothy Lull, *Martin Luther's Basic Theological Writings,* 183, 186 and 193.

4. Raymond Brown, *The Gospel According to John XIII-XXI*, 716.

5. Joel Green, *The Gospel of Luke*, New International Commentary on the New Testament. Grand Rapids: Eerdmans, 1997, p. 511.

6. Christ the King Sunday was inaugurated in 1925 by Pope Pius XI to counter the rise of secularism in which many were questioning the authority of Christ. In 1969 Pope Paul VI moved it from the end of October to the last Sunday in the liturgical year, to emphasize that starting in Advent we await the coming of the promised King, the Messiah.